Writing for the Soul:
An Autobiography & Guide for the Beaten Down

BY

Dylon J. Serpa

Dedication Page

I would like to thank everyone who supported me in

my struggles.

My Mother and Father (Dave and Gina Serpa)

All of my Grandparents

Gabi, Gabe, Jalen, Joey, Sean and Shawna

All of you supported me and I wouldn't have been able

to do it without you!

Disclaimer and Message

I am not a doctor or a psychologist and have nowhere near the knowledge these people have in their respective fields. I am not pretending to be a psychologist or saying I have the right to tell people how to deal with their mental health disorders. Not all of the sources in this book come from credible psychologists and again, these are just ways of helping you with the issues you run into, not professional advice. If you suffer from such problems as Depression, Anxiety, Schizophrenia or any related issues please see a counselor or take more serious action. If you or a person you know has been dealing with issues such as these take action! Make sure the people you care for do not go down the dark path that is mental health disorders. This book is simply a way of how to cope with your issues or methods to help. "Writing for the Soul" is in no way a means of diagnosing yourself. Again please seek help if you feel you are struggling through these *SERIOUS* problems. As someone who suffered through depression, please get the help you deserve! Now enjoy my story and hopefully you may relate. You may think your alone in this fight but you are not and if you take anything from this book I hope it is that you know someone cares somewhere out there! Numbers to call if needed:

1-800-273-TALK (Suicide Prevention Hotline)

1-630-482-9696 (Depression Hotline)

If you or a loved one would like to find a psychiatric hospital or call a counselor to schedule an appointment look in the local Yellow pages or go online and search for these, as needed.

The Problem and Why "Writing for The Soul"

Depression and mental health related diseases are a daunting problem in our society today and I would love to throw some stats into that brain of yours; according to the CDC over 14.8 million people in America alone suffer from depression and related disorders. In the American population the percentage of persons over the age of twelve taking prescription medication for mental health disorders is only 11% and instead of 1 out of 1 persons taking medication for mental health disorders only one out of three take medication to help them with their problems according to the CDC. Of those people taking prescriptions only one third of them have seen a mental health professional in the past year. Sixty percent of Americans who have taken medication for mental health disorders have been taking it for two years or longer and of those sixty, sixteen percent have taken it for ten years or longer, which is unacceptable, showing the problem carried on much longer than it should have even with medication. A whopping fifteen percent of kids between the ages of four through seventeen have had parents talk to a health professional or a health care provider about the behavioral struggles their child was having. Fifteen Percent! The estimated number of kids who have taken medication for behavioral difficulties is 2.9 million. The kids suffering from this monster need to be helped, we cannot allow children and teens to go undiagnosed or untreated for these issues, it simply is not okay.

The numbers are enormously scary when you are presented them; over thirty-eight thousand people committed suicide in the U.S. in 2010 according to the American Foundation for Suicide Prevention. Thirty-eight thousand people, who desperately needed help, tragically took their own lives in 2010. It's heartrending the way our society is not fully aware of the mental health issues surrounding us and we must take it upon ourselves to help the people in pain. According to the American Foundation for Suicide Prevention, since 1993 the rate of suicide has gone down in most years being at its lowest in 2000 when the suicide rate was only 10.5 out of 100,000 people but in recent years the rate has sky rocketed back up and reached a high point in 2010 when the rate rose to 12.5 out of 100,00 people. Here are some even scarier facts about suicide just in our own country (from AFSP website):

- Every 13.7 minutes someone in the United States dies by suicide.

- Nearly 1,000,000 people make a suicide attempt every year.

- 90% of people who die by suicide have a diagnosable and treatable psychiatric disorder at the time of their death.

- Most people with mental illness do not die by suicide.

- Recent data puts yearly medical costs for suicide at nearly $100 million (2005).

- Men are nearly 4 times more likely to die by suicide than women. Women attempt suicide 3 times as often as men.

  Please become aware of this issue and if you intend on attempting suicide then seek medical help. It is completely confidential and not one person will know besides you and your immediate family. *Do not become a statistic.*

The more statistics you see the more scary it becomes, "Approximately 80% of persons with depression reported some level of functional impairment because of their depression, and 27% reported serious difficulties in work and home life." The CDC said in 2005-2006. To continue on that the CDC also reported "Only 29% of all persons with depression reported contacting a mental health professional in the past year, and among the subset with severe depression, only 39% reported contact." Only 29% of people with depression contacted a health professional and only 39% of people with severe, clinical depression actually contacted a professional. It's astounding how little help people try to provide for themselves but that is why we, as a society, as a culture must help these people together and not allow them to go untreated.

Every person may feel sad or lonely every once in a while or for an extended period due to a loss or a unexpected life event but having clinical depression is a much more serious condition. There are plenty of warning signs or symptoms to spot; a constant sadness in someone, extreme pessimism, a person feeling guilty, hopelessness or no sense of self-worth, loss of appetite or heavy over eating, loss of interest in a previously passionate subject and these are just naming a few. The symptoms are obvious but what causes it and why? Anything can cause mental health disorders; losing a job, spouse, child or it simply could be hereditary, whatever the cause the disorders are real and people need to become aware of how it is destroying people from the inside out.

Now what are we going to do about it? How is the average Joe (not a Psychiatrist or Counselor) going to help a person who, most likely, does not want the help in any way, shape, or form? Simple tasks can be done to help a person you believe to be having these issues. Try holding interventions for the person you care about, with family and friends. Merely take the time to talk to the loved one about what's been going on lately, they will most likely open up about their problems without even realizing the fact. Do the person a favor and schedule an appointment with a therapist or counselor. By doing this you get your foot in the door, you allow them to know you have noticed something in their behavior and you want them to get the help they deserve. Most of the persons affected by these disorders will attempt to deny the fact they have an issue, they think their reputation with the community they dwell in or the status they hold with others will be hurt or lowered, when in circumstance, not one person will be opinionated on the matter. Not one person on this Earth should be allowed to walk around without help, everyone deserves it and not one person should go undiagnosed or unhealed, period!

"Writing for The Soul" might sound extremely odd but the basis is simple and basic; writing for the good of your soul. Numerous studies in the Psychology world have been going on for the past few decades or so and the shown benefits of writing therapy in people who have been diagnosed with a mental health disorder haven't disappointed yet. The aid writing is beginning to show in the recovery process for mental health disorders is beyond great. The supreme part about writing therapy is the writing can be done anywhere, anytime. Psychologists have even been able to help people through the mediums of e-mail or Internet services. The power therapeutic writing holds in the world is absolutely unbelievable, it has been said to have helped Vietnam War Veterans, mentally disturbed prison inmates and sex offenders with individual troubles they held in the past. A piece of paper can hold many faces, experiences, and problems. In the world of mental health disorders a piece of paper is no longer the weight of a feather but in turn the weight of a Whale.

My Journey

Before you come to know how "Writing for the Soul" is beneficial or how it will help you or a loved one with the struggles being faced I am going to share with you an autobiographical look on my childhood and my story. I believe you will come to see how important this really is and why I am backing it so firmly. The Journey I had taken through depression was exceptionally sad but I made my way out by being provided with a tool that became not just useful to me in depression but useful to me in everyday life.

As a child I was a fun loving kid who enjoyed having fun and enjoyed life. I smiled a lot, played a ton and was an overall great kid; anybody will tell you that but as a child I was a hefty kid. I had what most Moms would call "big-bones" and some of the kids in school were not very nice or passive of the fact. I was called the usual; fat, chubby, certain animal names and the words hurt me. I remember Johnny Depp's character Jack Sparrow, I'm sorry, CAPTAIN Jack Sparrow being ridiculed for something he had done in the movie Pirates of the Caribbean and he replied with an naive "sticks and stones, love!" Well, sorry to tell you Captain Jack but in reality "sticks and stones" certainly doesn't apply. When words come across you about appearance or certain related matters you become very insecure of yourself. On the outside you try to hold it together and you try to show you have the toughest skin possible but on the inside you die a little bit every time a bully or a person calls you names, it just hurts. Throughout elementary school the harassment continued, I ended up in various argumentative fights and even ended up in a few physical fights. On television being "big-boned" is glamourized particularly in sports, a big guy of six feet eight, two hundred and seventy five pounds is listed as an all-star when he gathers up fifteen sacks in a season or when he scores over thirty points per game but in school being large doesn't mean your in charge, it actually means quite the opposite, it means you're the bottom of the food chain; looking up at everyone else waiting for them to theoretically take a dump on your feelings and personal security. I became very insecure about my weight and looks. Everyday my Mom or Dad had to console me about the problem and it came to a point where I did not want to go to school anymore. School seemed like it was more of a grounds for me to be made fun of then a place of learning. It blew my mind that people would be so cruel and I found a way to vent through basketball and reading. All my days in the latter part of elementary school consisted of going to school, doing homework, playing basketball and reading. Reading honestly progressed me through some parts of my day and the allure of reading was the fact that I was able to transport away from the world to wherever I pleased. In James and the Giant Peach I rode that giant peach with James and his friends Mr. Grasshopper and Miss Spider on their whacky journey. I read books like The Chronicles of Narnia and Harry Potter because they allowed me to escape the world I live in. It truly helped and to this day I credit reading and writing as the main reason I escaped dreaded elementary school.

As the years went on the immaturity of elementary school went away and middle school brought forth bigger and better things, for the most part. The occasional bullying or joke was pulled on me but most everybody grew out of the fooling around. I breezed through middle school with virtually no problems, I had great grades and was in the top five percentile in reading for state standardize testing; my reading was considered post college level, and at a young age of twelve I really enjoyed knowing I was so prestigious in something I enjoyed.

High school was coming along and it was a scary thought to know I was going into the hot bed of immaturity. The stories you hear growing up about high school are utterly crazy; he did this, she did that, they ended up bullying the kid to death, I built up quite the high anxiety waiting for the beginning of high school due to my past with bullying.

The summer going into my freshman year I played basketball for Saint Bonaventure High School, the school I was going to be attending. I built great friendships with a number of players on the team and it seemed as though things were looking up for the most part; my grades were not perfect but were very good and basketball became a promising way of getting me to college. I built a strong relationship with the head Varsity coach and he believed in me much more than I did myself. He saw a potential in me that I never even saw once in myself and I thank him for showing me the ropes in basketball.

My freshman and sophomore years were easy as I breezed through them. School was going tremendously well and basketball was going along even better. As a sophomore I played Junior Varsity for my Dad and it was the best season of basketball I had ever played. I scored fifteen points a game to go along with five assists and in the summer going into my junior year I attended a basketball camp at Santa Clara University in Northern California, about a six hour drive from home. Every summer the team went up as a whole to play other schools at Santa Clara but the coaches invited me to come to their individual camp for five days of full on basketball. I had an outstanding camp and received the camp award for best shooter. My confidence was at an all time high after camp and I felt as though my junior year was going to be outstanding but in between the camp and the beginning of school something changed. I do not remember the exact day I began to feel funny but I do remember waking up in bed in the latter parts of summer feeling groggy, lethargic and disinterested in what the day held. It became worse as I started school; I began to lose interest in reading for the most part and would shun any reading assignments given by teachers. I remember being in English class, which of course was my absolute favorite subject and completely avoiding reading the book Into the Wild by Jon Krakauer. Before this day I never missed reading assignments on purpose. Maybe I missed an assignment here or there due to forgetfulness but that was an excuse acceptable to at least myself. Looking back on this happening I have come to notice this was the beginning of my issues with mental health and I sometimes regret not reading the odd and strange book hoping it could've changed the future a little bit. Basketball was still going well but where as I used to look forward to going to practice and weights I started making excuses to myself of why I shouldn't be going. The motivational motor installed into my brain by my Father was absolutely breaking down and it needed a tune-up quickly. Reminiscing, I even recall missing a few zero period (a school period for sports at 6 in the morning) workouts because I felt too lazy to go and I *never missed* one before my junior year.

My grades dropped dramatically during the second semester of my junior year. I went from having a few A's and B's to having C's, D's and F's in all of my classes, I took no interest in my classes or what warnings my teachers were conveying to me of not passing, I distanced myself from people more and more as the year went on and it was certainly becoming a mammoth of a problem, but I didn't care. I didn't even stop to think once about the damage I was doing to myself and my future. What confused me the most about what was going on with my life was how much I screamed for help but received none; nobody, not even my parents seemed to notice how much help I actually needed or asked for indirectly.

I recall a night where my parents and I were in the house talking about a family member who was struggling with depression heavily. My Father told me "If you ever feel like that you need to let us know, immediately." I stood there continuing what I was doing but on the inside screamed! How are you not noticing that I am feeling identical to that? Aren't my grades a big enough indication of how I am doing at the moment? Isn't showing absolutely no remorse for missing assignments or practices enough? Is waking up at 11:30 in the morning at least a little bit of an indication to you that I am not doing alright? Apparently none of these were big enough displays of how I was doing.

On the inside of me I noticed the changes I was going through, not just mentally, but physically as well. As I grew up year round basketball helped trim my body and I became a lot more thin than I had been as a young child in elementary school but as I developed less and less interests in things I became lazy and complacent making me gain tons of weight. I went from six three, two hundred and thirty pounds to about six four, two hundred and seventy pounds in a matter of months. By the end of my junior year I was a shell of the young man I was in my first two years of high school, not to mention my whole life, and to me it felt like no one cared.

During the summer going into my senior year of high school my school basketball team played in tournaments and leagues to get us in shape before the start of the school year. I had some rage built up inside due to the loss of control hovering over my life and I had a raging black out for the first time in one of our summer league games. We were in the city of Burbank, CA, about an hour away from where I lived (I was born in Burbank and it's where my grandmothers currently lived) for a summer league game at Burbank high school. Coach had suggested a player take the ball and I suggested my best friend Gabe take the ball during the overtime since he was playing so well on that particular day. Coach yelled, "If you want to be a coach then don't be a player! Go sit on the bench!" He continued to yell at me as I went to sit down, he would not shut up and from there things become very blurry; the rage inside of me built and built until I could not with hold it any longer, I recall kicking down the chair and storming out of the gymnasium with fury, destroying a couple of doors in the process. I don't remember much more but I do remember ending up about a block over from the school at a gas station asking the attendant if I could make a phone call. I called my Grandmother who came over to pick me up but as she drove up my Dad did as well and took me home. We did not talk much about the incident on the hour long drive but we did talk about what had caused it and all I said was "I don't know." I was in extreme denial about what was wrong with me, and for the life of me, I would not bring it up with anyone, not even my parents. After another incident my Mother worried about the status of my mental health due to a long list of family with mental health disorders and decided to take me to our family physician for help. He prescribed me a new medication that I do not remember the name of and we started treating me from there.

Several more happened throughout the summer and my most serious incident happened at Point Loma University in San Diego, CA. I remember completely leading the team through the game and by middle way through the second half I had scored about twenty-five points. My confidence was back and after starting the treatment of medication our family physician had prescribed I felt much better than I had in the previous weeks. The game was extremely close in the last minutes but near the two-minute mark my coach yanked me from the game for no apparent reason, he did it just to do it as far as I was concerned. I walked off the court quickly and snidely said, "I guess you want to lose now, right Coach?" (I regret saying those words to this day, the relationship I had with Coach dissolved from that point and was never the same again) I grabbed the bag of balls sitting at the end of the bench and threw them half way across the gym. I blistered up the stairs running half way through the parking lot before a very good man by the name of Mr. Baham, caught me and attempted to calm me down. Even though I might have never expressed to the man how much he helped me that night I thank him with all my heart. If he wouldn't have caught me I don't know where I would be today. He kept me at bay until my Mother and Father found me after the game. They were still in the gymnasium when I left, probably too embarrassed to run after their foolish, egotistical looking son.

The night the incident happened at Point Loma University I changed. I saw what I was doing and really never did it again. I had a few little out lashes during the season but really tried to not do it again because doing that made my school look bad as well as the team and it was unfair to my teammates and coaches the way I acted but I hope they can forgive me, I didn't have any control of my life at that point in time and they suffered through it just as much as I did. They put up with my crap for almost an entire year and even though they might have not helped me directly they helped me by showing support and not becoming angry with me about what I was doing.

Senior year rolled around and my life felt like shambles. Monday through Friday I made sure to make my parents lives a living hell by never getting out of bed to go to school. I would just lie there and not move. They tried everything to get me out of bed but nothing worked and my Mom, having her own past with depression, quickly acted on seeing certain symptoms and took me to see a counselor this time instead of our family physician. She asked me if I was continuing my prescription medication for my problems but I had stopped because it made me feel lethargic during basketball games. Even though I began seeing somebody to help me with my problems I still would not go to school because I wanted not one person to see me in the state I was living. Only my best friends saw me the way I was and I am so thankful for them. Each day I had my car I drove not to school but to a nearby park that resided only a block from my house. Every day I went to the park instead of school they messaged me on my phone and asked if I was ok or if I needed help. The dedication and loyalty they showed me was unbelievable, they exhibited the true meaning of friendship.

Having to live in a depressive state is most likely one of the worst things a person can go through in a lifetime. The feeling is one of the more empty feelings a person can ever encounter. Everyday you are tested mentally in a way not even comparable; I remember the feeling so vividly. Each night I would be wholly disappointed in myself (continuing the feeling of my self-worthlessness) that I had not gone to school or been as productive as I had wanted to throughout the day so I promised myself every night, "I am going to school tomorrow!" or "I need to do so and so, tomorrow." But when I woke up each morning my mind would shut down.

I remember laying in bed and in the back of my mind my conscious telling me, "Let's go Dylon you can do this, get out of bed and show the world that you can beat this!" My conscious screamed at me, it yelled for hours on end trying to get me up and out of bed but my body never moved. *I felt trapped in my own body*; it was the foulest I had ever felt in my entire life and there are ways I can describe to you the feeling but there are also *indescribable* ways of conveying the exact feelings and sensations of those mornings. Imagine yourself in a room with four walls and neither of those walls has a door leading out; you are left with huge tools to break down those walls but you can neither pick up those tools nor break down the walls with your bare hands. At some point you become so agitated and anxious you don't want to deal with life anymore. That explanation is truly the best I can give.

Those mornings were absolutely dreadful. Each day
I woke up I felt as though another piece of me had died.

It's funny how I remember this specific morning. My Mother tried and tried to get me to go to school, she physically was shoving clothes onto my body just trying to get me out of bed and out into the world but she pushed me too far. I stayed sitting at the end of the bed becoming aware of how mentally exhausted I was by the way I was living. She walked into the room and raised her voice "Dylon, go to school now! Let's go! Come on you can do this! Just get out of bed, go to school and feel better!"

I replied with "I am not going and stop telling me to go or I am going to drive off somewhere and *kill myself*!"

She hurried out of my room crying hysterically and immediately called my Father and the counselor I was seeing hoping we could all meet that day to discuss what was going on.

Now to be clear, I didn't intend on actually hurting myself, the thought had never even crossed my mind throughout the duration of my issues with depression but it was a message to her and everyone else around me. I needed big time help because I was growing weary of feeling the way I did. Life was not intended on being lived the way I was living; I needed to find a way to recover from what I was struggling with.

My counselor Amber (who I appreciate with all my heart) suggested in our meeting I write down everyday how I was feeling, the way I felt throughout the day and some other tricks like writing down daily goals, weekly goals and yearly goals for myself. I scoffed at writing down such petty things; I thought it was absolutely, one hundred percent senseless to write down these things. How was writing down goals or emotions going to help me recover from the pain I held within? Regardless of the high doubts I held, I decided to try it anyways and to my disbelief it truly worked.

In my counseling I found writing as a useful tool to positively direct my emotions and issues. It became an everyday habit; I would go through my day, take notes in my mind of what I went through throughout the day, then at the end of the day type out what I felt or what had transpired during the day, similar to a diary. I created a system that helped me whether it was writing down the happenings of the day or a story idea that developed in my head.

Writing became an addictive drug to me. I wrote about anything my mind could grasp! It became somewhat soothing for me, it became not just a tool to help me with the problems I was having but ultimately became an aspiration of mine. After a few months of writing I actually wanted to become a writer, an author, I wanted to show the world my talents and it has worked out great so far. I have a recently published children's book called "Moosey's Adventures: The Way Home" and am working on having the second book of the series published but I wanted to do more with my writings. I wanted to help the cause I suffered from and show others the immense powers of therapeutic writing. Writing can aid to whomever is struggling and, again, the best part of writing is it can be done anytime, anywhere with no restraints.

I hope sharing my story with you has helped you feel a better connection to me and understand when you fall into that deep pit; you can crawl out, it might be tough, it could take a lot of time but when you do edge out from the dark hole and into the light you see how beautiful the world really is.

I sometimes find myself starring at a magnificent sunset or looking at the world around me in disbelief. When I was in the depressive state I was in, everything was black and white like an old television show. No color was present in my world. For that reason I wake up everyday, throw the covers off of myself, get out of bed, walk over to the blinds and quickly draw them upwards.

Light and color instantly fills the room and I take a deep breath of fresh air, just being happy to be healthy furthermore awake.

My girlfriend Hunter once told me this "I can never find out when you're serious because you're always smiling", while she didn't necessarily mean this in a good way, I took it as that. I smile everyday, every moment because of the dark stages I went through. Every chance you have, smile. Smiling not only brightens your world but others as well. You never know of how a smile may change another person's life. I once read a story in a book about this young man who had been bullied for much of his life because he was a "dork", "geek" and really just an intelligent boy who didn't necessarily socialize very well. One day he planned of killing himself after school because he was fed up with life and could not stand any more ridicule or suffering. School ended and he began literally walking to his death but a student from school walked up to him on his walk and smiled while asking him what he was up to. The boy who was going to kill himself was walked home by this student and ended up not committing suicide due to what this other student had done. It was a touching story and I keep that story close to my heart especially when I see someone being mocked or bullied. I always put a smile on my face for others because you will never know how it may help, a smile could mean a million new beginnings to another person.

Where I am today; in college, an author and an overall great person I credit to the support I had while going through the problems I encountered. Without the support of friends and family I would be nowhere near where I am now. Having a great support team is positively *crucial* to solving the tribulations you are having but *remember that you always have the necessary tools within yourself to beat whatever it is you are going to beat.*

Writing exercises

You may not know where to start with writing you may not even know how to write but it is okay because again the beauty of writing is that it can be done anytime, anywhere and by *anyone.*

People have kept journals for years; girls especially love to write down their life into the journal they own, it is a very secretive part of a person's life. You can write down thoughts, feelings, really anything of importance to the life you are living and I urge you to start by keeping a daily log. Where the daily log differs from the journal is the way you write and what you write inside of the log. A daily log is a tool very useful to many and proved to be extremely useful to me; throughout the day go ahead and write down the ways you have felt, the emotions you feel and the way you act. Put the log down for a short period of time and go back to look at it, by doing this you will see the way you act or feel. It becomes a personal checks and balances system where you begin to see how erratic your behavior is becoming. In these log entries you want to stray away from an outside or external point of view; the words you put down have to be internal thoughts and experiences. Releasing your thoughts onto the paper will allow the weight to be lifted from your shoulders a bit. The emotions will not magically disappear but it will ease the stress of what you are feeling. By performing the daily entries you come to understand your problems in better understanding and instead of sulking on the issues you try to solve them; you become *proactive*. A great exercise you are able to do in these logs is write five things down that went well for you during the day, every night before you go to bed. This will allow you to point out the sweeter things going on in life instead of the bad. Being able to appreciate the little stuff in life is a strong focus in therapeutic writing; writing is about bringing out all the *good* never the bad. Writing therapy follows the old adage "It's the finer things in life."

An exercise you may want to start out with is an introduction story about yourself in a positive manner; the story may be as long as you possibly like. In the writings give a solid description about yourself and how you are at your highest confidence level and do not forget to make yourself the main character. If you are feeling extra creative then try turning it into a full fictitious story, try turning the life you live into a story like Twilight, Hunger Games or Harry Potter, try flipping the life you live into the most incredible story you have ever read. When you finish composing the story have another person read it and tell you the strengths about the main character within the story. It allows you to hear what you think of yourself and aids in knowing another person agrees with the strengths pointed out inside of the story. You always want to hear strengths, never demean yourself or put yourself down. You're worth a damn and have talents that can be utilized.

Another trick I learned while going through my writing therapy was a trick called the "trash theory". I developed the idea while listening to my friend speak of something he does with text messages and e-mails when upset or exhausted by a certain person. He would write out this extensive e-mail or text message explaining to the person exactly how he felt, it could say "I hate you" or "I hope you burn in hell" but whatever the message he always deleted it when he felt he had released the anger he had toward the individual. I took what he did with messages and applied it to my everyday writing regiment hoping it would help. Do not use your daily log for this, grab a piece of disposable paper and write down how you truly feel about a person or situation. When you feel you have forced all your opinions and problems onto the page crumble up the paper and forcefully throw it into the trashcan. The feeling when throwing away the piece of paper is a feeling of triumph; it's the same feeling as when passing an important test. It gives you the sense of finishing unfinished business and it is one of the more relieving exercises I have put myself through. I recommend the "trash theory" over all of the other exercises, hands down. And do not forget to throw the wadded up ball of paper *forcefully*, I mean you have to really throw it in there!

A more fun activity to do before you fall asleep is the "dream writing" activity. Take one of the "good" occurrences that happened to you during the day and try writing, in a positive manner, about the "good" occurrence as it was a dream you were having. Give this occurrence a short name then lie down in bed and visualize the happening over and over. This should help for more positive dreams and more positive dreams allows for a better outlook on life, you will find yourself being more optimistic about all aspects of life. Just as writing is a powerful tool for a more optimistic life so are dreams, scientist speak of how dreams are the key to our subconscious and by doing this exercise you will find out how much of that is true.

A blog by the name of "Outkast" has a great suggestion about an exercise from famous psychologist

Karen Reivich "For many of us, anger is an emotion we experience far too often. Small things become huge betrayals. Betrayals become crimes. We hold onto our grudges. Anger and resentment often lead to dwelling on them and fantasies about how to get back at the person who hurt us. It is easy to lose sight of the whole person and to only focus on what the person did to hurt you. When this happens, the anger crowds out positive emotions and you hang on to the grudge. The grudges exercise is designed to help you let go of your grudges. It uses gratitude to loosen your grip on the grudge. The goal of the exercise is NOT to excuse, forget or minimize what happened to you, but to see the other person in their entirety and to remember and record as many things as you can for which you are grateful to them. By shifting your focus from grudge to gratitude, the anger you feel decreases and your perspective becomes broad again.

Perhaps one way this exercise works is that the gratitude "undoes" the effects of anger. Hanging onto anger does not help you to move forward in your life. It makes you feel worse and keeps you from thinking about good things and focusing on your goals.

Choose a person in your life that you know well and have a grudge against. On a piece of blank paper, draw a circle in the center of the page and record a few words that capture the essence of the grudge.

Then, fill the rest of the page with blank circles – at least 15 of them. The object is for you to fill each of these circles with a word or phrase that describes something about the person for whom you are grateful – something he/she said to you, did for you, something important about the relationship, small things, big things, current things, historical things.

After you have filled in each of the circles, hold the page at arms distance and notice how the grudge gets lost in the sea of gratitude.

Write on how your emotions and thoughts change as you focus on the person now. Are you able to see the person more fully? Do your feelings for the other person change in any way? Does the importance and meaning of the wrong doing change? Are you in a better position to talk with the person about the hurtful event (if that is safe or necessary)? Are you in a better position to problem solve? Are there positive parts of the relationship that you now remember and would like to focus on and cultivate or grow? Do you notice any changes in how your mood and how you feel about yourself?

Note: You can also do this exercise by drawing the shape of trees instead of circles. You fill in the center tree with the grudge and then fill in all of the other trees with "gratitude's". We use this format with students and then ask them to think about how the grudge tree makes them lose sight of the forest of things for which they are grateful."

There is so much in this quote about not only the exercise you are doing but also of relationships in general. When you have the problems of facing a mental health disorder the emotions in any given situation are multiplied by ten. Holding a grudge towards someone you know and possibly love can turn into an entirely different problem, maybe ending in a violent dispute. The exercise given here is a exceptionally helpful tool that allows you to see past the struggles of a relationship, allowing you to *forgive* and *forget*.

Following the reading of how to perform this exercise I related to it heavily. When I was struggling with my issues of blacking out, I seemed not to care who was trying to restrain me or calm me down, I once even punched my father square in the chin during a dispute in the locker room during a basketball game and I love my Dad to death. In a normal and sane state of mind I would never, ever punch my Father but because of the issues entangled in my life I did hurt him physically and was extremely remorseful for it. Having such an exercise to help you with such a boundless subject, as grudge is a tremendous tool and should be used as much as it possibly can be used when dealing with bitterness. You may find writing the fifteen circles is quite difficult due to the fact of you focusing on the problems the person may have caused you but try to put the problems aside and truthfully do the exercise. You will come to find that grudge does turn to gratitude. The exercise really proves to be worthwhile when doing it about family members, especially parents.

I attended a catholic high school and a trip we took every year, as a class was an annual retreat. My senior year a few teachers arranged for us to go up into the cabins in the mountains about an hour and a half away from the school. The whole weekend was emotionally powerful, something I had never really experienced before and being in such solitude with my fellow classmates drew me closer to them somehow. The night before the end of the retreat our retreat leader Scott Boczek (this man is truly a living saint and may I do him justice by pronouncing his name correctly [Bo-Zach]) handed us all letters from our parents or legal guardians. We all had no clue this was going to occur and I believe everyone was in more shock reading these letters than they ever had been. Scott reached out to each one of our parents asking for a confidential letter explaining to us how much we mean to our parents and whatever else our parents wanted to say to us. I can easily say it was one of the more touching moments in my lifetime. I looked up from my letter and came to find myself drowning my t-shirt in tears and I am in no way, shape or form a crier. Slightly embarrassed, I looked around the room to make sure I wasn't the only person crying, to my surprise I found not one dry eye in the room. One hundred percent of the people in the room were crying and what professionals call this letter is a "healing" letter. You may choose to write one yourself (as many as you would like) to any person who has caused you pain in the past. The choice of sending the letter or not is a choice you will make but writing the words down to describe the pain the person has caused you will be justice enough. Following the exercise of you sending the letter write an imaginary response letter in the point of view of the person who caused you the pain. What you need to write is how you believe the person would respond to your letter and write down something you also want to hear from them about what they had done to you in the past whether that be abuse, bullying, etc. This exercise will allow you to seal the experience of having the feeling of uncompleted business between yourself and that person who caused you the pain you suffer from.

A useful exercise I found online is the "mirror exercise". Stare at yourself in front of a mirror; do not rush this part, it may be mentally difficult to stare at yourself in a mirror but remember this is for the good of you. Take a deep breath and write down what you see or how you feel *without* using the pronoun *"I"*. Answer such questions as you are another person and answer questions like, how do I feel about this person? Is this person a good person or not? Is this person trustworthy? How would you feel meeting this person, would it be a good first impression? You will learn more about yourself in the ten or twenty minutes you look at yourself in the mirror than you have in a few years. I tried this exercise and while it was extremely challenging to take a hard look at myself in the mirror I came to be impressed by the way I saw myself. Most of the comments I had for myself were very optimistic and I even added in some helpful tips for myself about what I could do better or improve in my life.

Another habit I learned in counseling was putting my troubles behind me for a quick minute and imagining my life in a successful manner. I would always imagine myself playing basketball at the University of California Los Angeles (UCLA) studying Journalism and then graduating from UCLA with a Bachelor's Degree and continue on to report as a sports journalist for ESPN.

Those days were the days I dreamed of in high school and obviously my dreams have changed since then but while I was in counseling they inspired me. Try to keep yourself in a meditative state for a few minutes and imagine your life with no restraints, no issues. Concluding the mediation write down what you see. What are the goals you hold for yourself? Where would you like your life to be in a few years and how do you want to be living that life? What career path do you want to take? After writing all of these answers down make copies of this paper full of goals and put it on the front and back of your bedroom door, on the ceiling above your bed; put the piece of paper anywhere you are going to definitely see it. This will allow you to see the goals you have and strive for them. When you wake up and are feeling blue, take a look at the goals you set for yourself, it will give you the strength and motivation to get your butt out of bed and into school or work.

For people who are a little more inspired spiritually try an exercise pointed out by a respected blog named "The Bruised Muse": "For this exercise, imagine you're walking down the road one fine day. Or you could be in your kitchen and there's a knock at the door, or at your desk, or on the bleachers watching your child's hockey game, or sitting down at your desk. You choose the setting, which I hope you will describe with as many sensory details as you can. And suddenly a person comes up to you whom you somehow recognize as God. What does God look like? Describe God's appearance. I'm not necessarily looking for flowing robes, white beards and symbols of religion here, because presumably God can take any form. Choose one that has meaning to you: someone you know or don't know, someone from your past or future, your dead child or sister, Morgan Freeman, George Burns, your long lost Aunt, a Buddhist monk. What is he wearing? What does he look like? You get to have a conversation with God. Don't hold back. God can take whatever you dish out. And you say to God, "Why me?" And God says, "Why not you?"

Write the scene complete with dialogue from there. Try to get past any nervousness you have about talking to God, and even consider challenging God. For example, if you don't like God's answer, say so. As always, feel free to write this from someone else's point of view, either in the first person or third. Do this for seven minutes."

While I am not too spiritual you might be and it could possibly be one of the more healing exercises you find. Religion and spirituality are enormously respected healers and pain relievers, which is the exact reason I recommend this exercise. Tons of people have found salvation in a specific religion; they find god, become Buddhist, or Muslim but the shear impact of each of those religions have on a person's life is significant enough to want to make change for the good of themselves. Some of the more religious people have amazing, positive outlooks on the life they live and a positive outlook is all you really need to overcome!

Another Story

A second story I would like to share with you is the one of my thirteen-year-old cousin. She came down with the symptoms of having terrible depression and anxiety. Each day I would hear more news from my Mother about the condition she was in or the way she was feeling and it completely tore my heart to shreds. I have watched her grow into a young woman and seeing her begin to go through what I went through just made me angry at life and sad that such a smart, talented, exuberant young lady was having such troubles.

Eventually my cousin ended up in a hospital about an hour away from home. She was not doing very well and after about a week stay was eventually sent home when our family and the doctors believed she was ready to. A day after she was sent home I took it upon myself to send her a letter (I am not a great face to face conservationist) because I felt as though it was my *duty* to show her how I related and how I dealt with what she was dealing with. I told her the ways of how writing helped me and how they could possibly help her out as well.

The week after she was sent home I drove up north to the Modesto area for my Uncle's wedding and saw her the next day. I remember seeing a few things in her that I had seen in myself; not talkative, spacing herself from socializing and she just looked tired, very, very tired. I could see her struggling with whatever she was struggling with. If I may say so again, the feeling of being clinically depressed is one of the most dreadful and awful things a human being can be put through and seeing such a young teenager going through that was just heartbreaking. My Aunt assured me the letter was sent to my cousin and I felt well knowing she might find some sort of solace in writing.

A few months after these problems arose she started doing better due to the help of medication and counseling and I was able to see her when we again went up to Northern California for my Aunt's 40th birthday party. I was apart of a ton of great things that night; I saw my Aunt get completely hammered (awesome), I was able to spend time with my cousin Gabi (she is like a sister to me) and I was able to spend time with my beloved Girlfriend Hunter but the most beautiful thing I laid eyes on that night was my thirteen-year-old cousin writing something down in a journal. It was heart warming to know she took my advice on writing and the help it can bring you in facing the issues in front of you. For the purposes of this book I asked her what she thought of writing, furthermore how it helped her face these challenges. She gave me perhaps the best quote to sum up the entirety of this book "Uhm, it's like I can express myself without being judged. Or, like it takes out my anger or sadness. It's an escape from this world and into somebody else's."

Hearing this warmed my heart once again; what she put into words I have been trying to put into words since I began writing. The feeling you acquire from writing is unrivaled by any other extracurricular. When she stated "…it's like I can express myself without being judged." I wholly agreed. The words you write are your words and your words alone, not anybody else's. Writing is all your own and a bully, a parent, or an annoying teacher at school cannot take that from you. Those were the wisest words I had ever heard come from the mouth of an early teenager and because of the trials my little cousin faced she is much more special and wise than any other person her age. I hope she knows how much respect I hold for her, I would never have been able to handle the problems I did at such an early age just as she did and it is astounding, no, remarkable that she was able to deal with it as she did. I thank her for allowing me to share her story with the world, I get to brag about my little cousin to the entire world and show how significant of a person she truly is to not just me but to the world and I believe she will be a very special person to society someday.

More Writing Exerices

As I said before a daily log is a necessity for therapeutic writing and these are some topics to do a daily log on:

- What is a necessity in your life and what do you need to flush out of your life?
- Most importantly, Rate ten things that bring you the most *Joy* in your life.
- What fears do you hold for yourself?
- Do you strive for certain successes or look for certain goals in your future?
- In your life what causes you the most sadness?
- What can you control in life and what can you not control?

- Are there things in your life you feel as though you do not need to fight for?

- Do you feel stuck in a rut or feel as though you cannot get passed one obstacle?

- Are there certain ways you are able to push yourself when down? Are there ways you create worse problems for yourself?

- What causes you to become the green monster? What are you jealous of?

- Write down dreams you have had recently, are they optimistic, pessimistic or neutral? How do you think life is affecting the dreams you are having?

- Are you happy with your life right now?

- Do you have any regrets about past relationships or problems you have not resolved?

- What excites you the most about life? Why do you want to keep living? Whether that be sports, family, loved one etc.

- Are there any specific extracurricular activities that help you out in the times you feel blue?

    "Writing for Self exploration" by Doctor Allan G. Hunter, says this about what to write:

- Simply put down whatever comes to your mind first, don't think about your response.

- In fact, don't think about what you've put down at all until the instructions tell you to.

- *Don't judge what you wrote, or use it as a way to put yourself down.*

- *Do HAVE FUN!*

    The fun aspect may be the most important aspect of writing for therapeutic need. If writing thrills you, aids you and allows you to come to life than do it. Do not let anyone tell you different. Remember to have fun with it and never forget that what you write is not theirs it is *yours*. What you write is never senseless, it's a unique and timeless masterpiece only *you* have written.

Lastly

Mental health disorders are an extremely important subject in our society today and I would be lying to you to say it's easy to beat because it certainly is not. You have to get yourself out of bed everyday with the motivation to say, "I will not let this take me down. This will be the day I overcome and conquer."

I enjoy reading about old Latin phrases, especially of war. Too be honest everything sounds much more epic in the ancient language and ten times more fun to attempt to say. A Latin phrase I really related to goes like this, ***"non omnis moriar."*** This simply translates to "Not all of me shall die." I share so much of my being in this particular phrase because of the issues I faced. Yes it may have cost me a great senior year in high school or it may have cost me a chance at going to a better college straight out of high school but it certainly did not take all of me, my true self did not die with what I faced and I am a better person for it today.

If you stuck me on a deserted island with my loved ones and a typewriter I could live in peace forever. As much as I loathed having a mental health disorder such as depression, I thank it in some ways. It drew out my passion of writing and allows me to help others who suffer from it, as well. Writing may be the key for so many people who suffer from mental health illness just as I did and that is why I shared this book with the world. If even one person is helped by the stories and suggestions in this book than I did what I was put on this Earth for, helping others. I believe the depression I suffered from put me in a better place in my life by showing me how writing could help me and therefore showed me a way to help others. I request that you as well as others around you share this with the world, so other people suffering from Depression and other health related issues may find a way to help themselves. We as a society will not allow this monster to destroy anymore lives than it already has, from 1993 through 2010 554,651 people have committed suicide due to mental health disorders, that is completely unacceptable. Writing is just a tool of how to find a way through depression but if anything else may bring you joy than do what brings you joy.

Writing is like water, as it can take any form at any given point in time, anywhere; that's the beauty of writing. Instead of leaving you with a boring old age Latin phrase I will leave you with the wise words of my younger cousin, "it's like I can express myself without being judged. Or, like it takes out my anger or sadness. It's an escape from this world and into somebody else's."

Daily Log

The next nine pages are all your own. What you do with them is solely up to how you would like to use them. If you decide to keep a daily log for the next 9 days then do so. If you would like to write the best damn nine-page fiction novel a person has ever put down on paper, then go for it. All I want for you is to begin writing in a productive and useful manner, so go ahead and write, write, write!

.

www.ingramcontent.com/pod-product-compliance
Lightning Source LLC
Chambersburg PA
CBHW050431290526
45786CB00003B/1483